D1074535

COUNTRY PROFILES

SOUTH AFRICA

BY ALICIA Z. KLEPEIS

BLASTOFF!
DISCOVERY

BELLWETHER MEDIA • MINNEAPOLIS, MN

Blastoff! Discovery launches a new mission: reading to learn. Filled with facts and features, each book offers you an exciting new world to explore!

BLASTOFF! UNIVERSE

BLASTOFF! Beginners — GRADE K

BLASTOFF! READERS — GRADES 1-3

BLASTOFF! DISCOVERY — GRADE 4

This edition first published in 2021 by Bellwether Media, Inc.

No part of this publication may be reproduced in whole or in part without written permission of the publisher.
For information regarding permission, write to Bellwether Media, Inc., Attention: Permissions Department,
6012 Blue Circle Drive, Minnetonka, MN 55343.

Library of Congress Cataloging-in-Publication Data

Names: Klepeis, Alicia, 1971- author.
Title: South Africa / by Alicia Z. Klepeis.
Other titles: Blastoff! discovery. Country profiles.
Description: Minneapolis : Bellwether Media, 2021. | Series: Blastoff!
   discovery. Country profiles | Includes bibliographical references
   and index. | Audience: Ages 7-13 | Audience: Grades 4-6 |
   Summary: "Engaging images accompany information about South
   Africa. The combination of high-interest subject matter and narrative
   text is intended for students in grades 3 through 8"–Provided
   by publisher.
Identifiers: LCCN 2020001623 (print) | LCCN 2020001624
   (ebook) | ISBN 9781644872581 (library binding) | ISBN
   9781681037219 (ebook)
Subjects: LCSH: South Africa–Juvenile literature.
Classification: LCC DT1719 .K55 2021 (print) | LCC DT1719 (ebook)
   | DDC 968–dc23
LC record available at https://lccn.loc.gov/2020001623
LC ebook record available at https://lccn.loc.gov/2020001624

Editor: Kieran Downs   Designer: Brittany McIntosh

Printed in the United States of America, North Mankato, MN.

TABLE OF CONTENTS

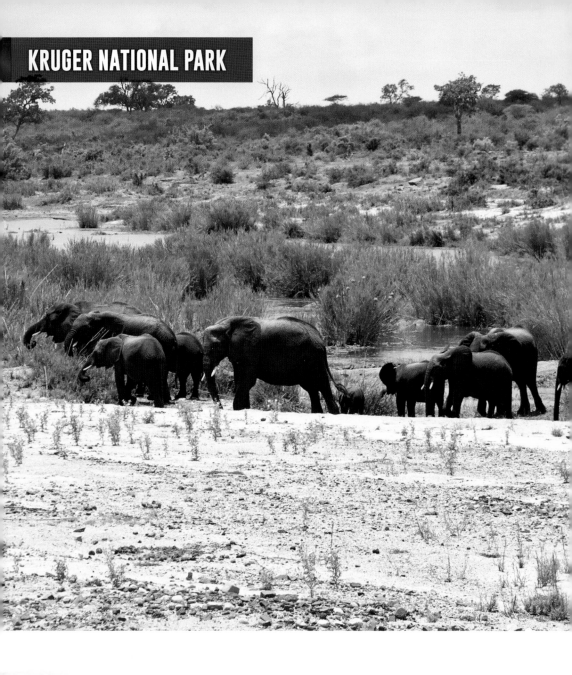

It is a warm afternoon at Kruger National Park.
A family boards a **safari** vehicle with open sides.
As they move past a herd of impala, the driver suddenly
stops. In the distance, a lion rests under a tree. His bushy
mane blows in the breeze.

OTHER TOP SITES

BLYDE RIVER CANYON NATURE RESERVE

THE GARDEN ROUTE

KIRSTENBOSCH NATIONAL BOTANICAL GARDEN

TABLE MOUNTAIN

Farther down the road, they arrive at the Sabie River. A white rhino bathes in the water. Yellow village weaver birds make a racket from their hanging nests. Later, the family discovers a group of elephants feeding on plants by the river's edge. Welcome to South Africa!

ZIMBABWE

BOTSWANA

NAMIBIA

PRETORIA

JOHANNESBURG

BLOEMFONTEIN

LESOTHO

SOUTH
AFRICA

PORT ELIZABETH

CAPE TOWN

ATLANTIC
OCEAN

PRINCE EDWARD ISLANDS

South Africa's Prince Edward Islands are located in the
southern Indian Ocean. They are about 1,200 miles
(1,931 kilometers) southeast of Cape Town.

MOZAMBIQUE

ESWATINI

DURBAN

INDIAN
OCEAN

PRINCE EDWARD
ISLANDS

South Africa is located on Africa's southern tip. The country covers 470,693 square miles (1,219,090 square kilometers). It has three capital cities. Pretoria is in northeastern South Africa. Bloemfontein sits in the center. Cape Town lies along the southwestern coast.

The Indian Ocean washes upon South Africa's eastern and southern coasts. Waves of the Atlantic Ocean crash onto its western shores. Namibia, Botswana, and Zimbabwe are South Africa's northern neighbors. Mozambique and Eswatini lie to the east. The small nation of Lesotho sits inside South Africa's borders.

N
W + E
S

7

Most of South Africa is made up of a huge **plateau**. The Kalahari Desert sits on the northern part of the plateau. The grassy Highveld is the plateau's largest region. The plateau is highest in the east and slopes down toward the west. The Great **Escarpment** is a mountainous region that surrounds the plateau. It includes the Drakensberg range in southern and eastern South Africa.

N
W+E
S

▨ = HIGHVELD   ▨ = KALAHARI DESERT
▨ = GREAT ESCARPMENT

THE ORANGE RIVER

The Orange River is the longest in South Africa. It starts in the Lesotho Highlands and flows into the Atlantic Ocean. The river is named after the royal Dutch house of Orange.

KALAHARI DESERT

CAPE TOWN
Average
seasonal highs
and lows

JANUARY
HIGH: 83 °F (28 °C)
LOW: 63 °F (17 °C)

APRIL
HIGH: 77 °F (25 °C)
LOW: 59 °F (15 °C)

JULY
HIGH: 68 °F (20 °C)
LOW: 52 °F (11 °C)

OCTOBER
HIGH: 76 °F (24 °C)
LOW: 58 °F (14 °C)

°F = degrees Fahrenheit
°C = degrees Celsius

Most of South Africa has a dry, **temperate** climate.
The eastern part of the country gets more rain than the west.
Cold ocean currents bring fog to the Atlantic coastline.

South Africa is a country with **diverse** wildlife. Great white sharks hunt for Cape fur seals and dolphins along the coasts. In the Kalahari Desert, giraffes feed on thorny acacia trees as springboks graze on shrubs and grasses. Cape cobras hunt for prey in the hot African sun.

South Africa is home to several **endangered** animals. Many of these animals live in national parks or on private game reserves. The areas provide rhinos, elephants, African wild dogs, and cheetahs with safety from human hunters.

GIRAFFES

AFRICAN WILD DOG

AFRICAN PENGUINS

African penguins make their homes in the cold coastal waters of South Africa. Their dense, waterproof feathers keep them dry and warm.

CHEETAH

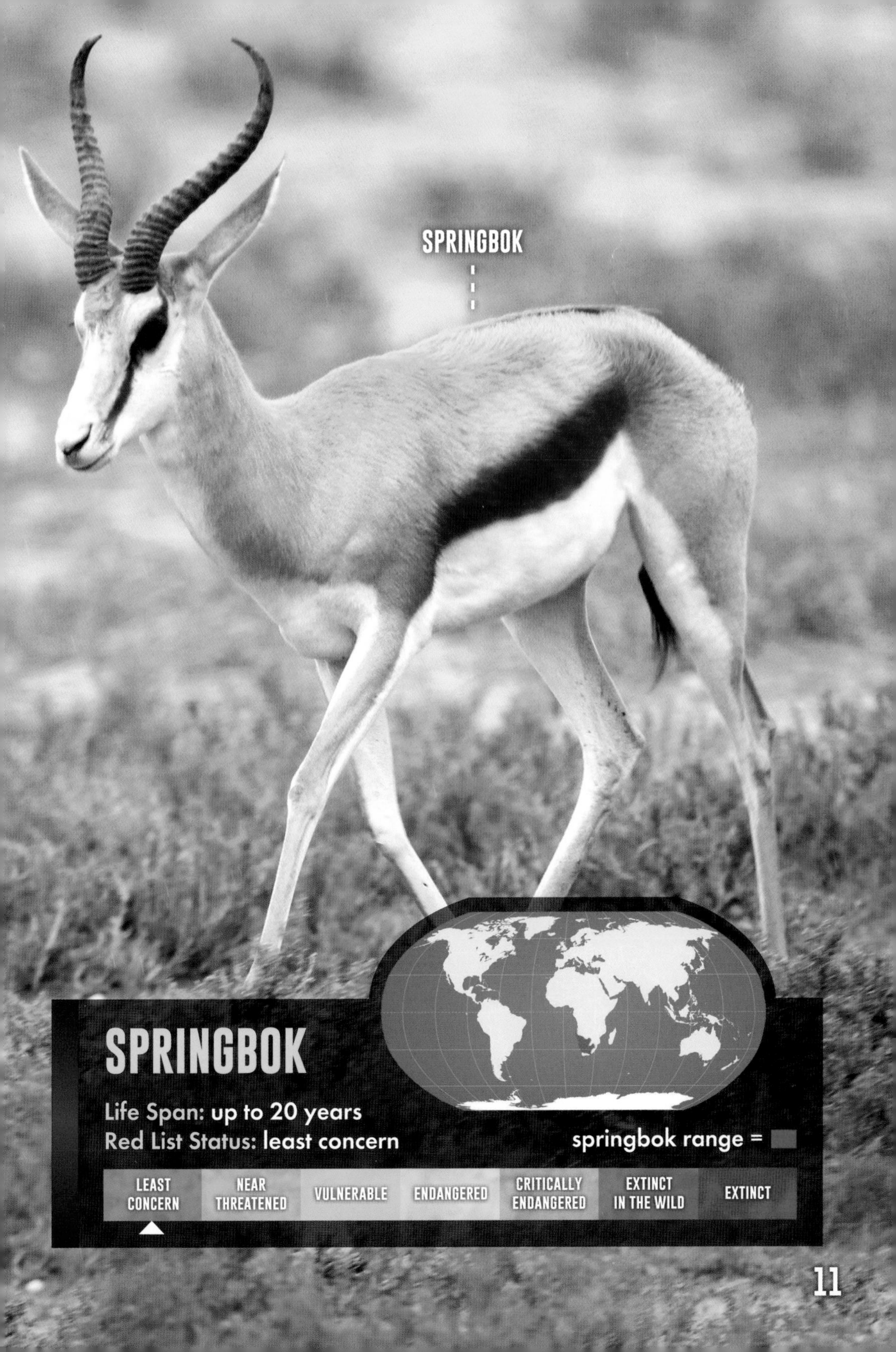

SPRINGBOK

SPRINGBOK

Life Span: **up to 20 years**
Red List Status: **least concern**

springbok range =

LEAST CONCERN	NEAR THREATENED	VULNERABLE	ENDANGERED	CRITICALLY ENDANGERED	EXTINCT IN THE WILD	EXTINCT
▲						

Over 56 million people live in South Africa. About four out of five people are black Africans. The second biggest group is people of mixed background. Fewer than one out of ten people in the country are white.

South Africa does not have an official religion. However, most people are Christian. Other South Africans practice **traditional** African religions or Islam. The country has eleven official languages. Zulu is the most widely spoken. Xhosa and Afrikaans also have many **native** speakers. It is common for people to speak at least two different languages in South Africa.

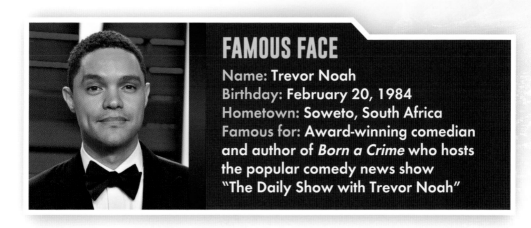

FAMOUS FACE

Name: Trevor Noah
Birthday: February 20, 1984
Hometown: Soweto, South Africa
Famous for: Award-winning comedian and author of *Born a Crime* who hosts the popular comedy news show "The Daily Show with Trevor Noah"

SPEAK ZULU

ENGLISH	ZULU	HOW TO SAY IT
hello	sawubona	sow-BOH-nah
goodbye	hamba kahle	HAM-bah gah-shey
please	ngicela	nee-keh-lah
thank you	ngiyabonga	gee-yah-BOHN-gah
yes	yebo	YEH-boh
no	cha	tah

CAPE TOWN

South African cities are crowded. About two out of three South Africans live in **urban** areas. Communities continue to be affected by **apartheid**. White people often live in single-family homes similar to the United States and Europe. Many people of color live in **informal settlements** created during apartheid. These **shantytowns** often lack running water and electricity. Minibuses are a popular way to get around for all city dwellers.

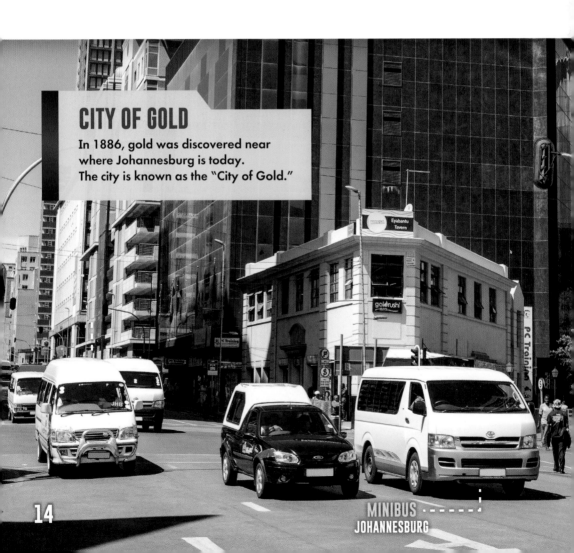

CITY OF GOLD

In 1886, gold was discovered near where Johannesburg is today. The city is known as the "City of Gold."

MINIBUS - - - - - - -
JOHANNESBURG

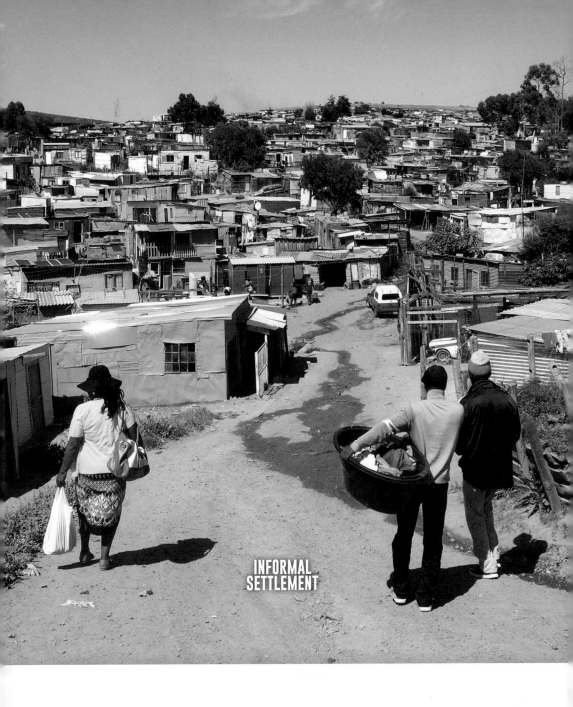

INFORMAL
SETTLEMENT

Rural houses are often traditional round huts. They have **thatched roofs**. People in the countryside often travel on foot, by bicycle, by animal, or by private vehicle.

CUSTOMS

DON'T SAY GOODBYE

Most farewell phrases in South Africa indicate that people will meet again. In English, they might say "see you." In Afrikaans, they could say *tot siens*, meaning "until we see each other again."

Family is very important to South Africans. People often live with extended family. The father is traditionally the head of the household. Grandparents might live with their children and grandchildren. They may help with childcare and earn money to support the family.

Music in South Africa comes in many varieties. Gospel and traditional folk songs are both popular. Many young South Africans listen to *kwaito* music. It includes African lyrics with a mixture of African, hip-hop, reggae, and house music. People across the country enjoy jazz, too.

JAZZ MUSICIANS

Children in South Africa start school at age 7. They are required to attend school until grade nine. Children tend to be educated in a local language until grade seven. After that time, they are usually taught in English. Secondary education is optional and typically includes career training. South Africa has many excellent colleges and universities.

More than 7 out of 10 South Africans have **service jobs**. Some work in restaurants, shops, or national parks. **Tourism** employs many people. South African workers **manufacture** products including cars and chemicals. Farmers grow corn, wheat, and citrus fruits.

FARMER

GOING DOWN

Mining provides a lot of jobs in South Africa. Some mines are very deep, reaching 2.5 miles (4 kilometers) below the earth's surface. Temperatures can reach more than 140 degrees Fahrenheit (60 degrees Celsius) in these mines.

RUGBY

Soccer, rugby, and cricket are all popular sports in South Africa. Children frequently play soccer on open spaces near their homes. The country's national rugby team, the Springboks, won the 2019 Rugby World Cup. Swimming and tennis are also popular sports.

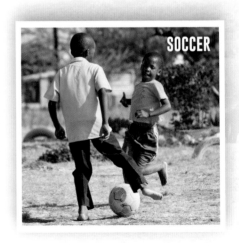

SOCCER

South Africans tend to spend their free time outdoors. Beaches can become quite crowded during school vacations or on weekends. People also hike or have picnics in local parks. Popular indoor activities include going to the movies or shopping with friends. South Africans commonly dance and go to concerts.

HIKING

SOUTH AFRICAN ANIMAL SILHOUETTES

People visiting Africa's national parks often take photos of amazing animals at sunset. Create your own animal silhouette by sunset scene!

What You Need:
- white construction paper
- black construction paper
- orange, red, yellow tissue paper
- a pencil
- scissors
- a ruler
- a glue stick

Instructions:
1. Draw the outline of an animal that lives in South Africa onto the black construction paper. Use scissors to cut it out.

2. Choose one color of tissue paper for the background of your sunset. Glue the tissue paper to a piece of white construction paper.

3. Cut two or three 1.5-inch (4-centimeter) wide strips of tissue paper from each of the non-background colors of tissue paper.

4. Glue these strips onto the background sunset color near the middle of the page to add color to the sunset.

5. Glue the silhouette of your animal onto the sunset background.

6. You can cut out the shape of a tree or round hut from the black paper and add it to your scene. Be creative!

21

DELICIOUS DESSERTS

South Africa has a lot of different desserts. *Malva* pudding is a sweet and spongy cake. *Koeksisters* are similar to glazed donuts, except they have a braided shape.

Most South African **cuisine** features corn and other vegetables. *Mealie pap* is a popular cornmeal porridge. It is eaten as a sweet breakfast or a side dish. People often liven up meals with a vegetable dish called *chakalaka*. It includes tomatoes, onions, peppers, carrots, beans, and spices.

Commonly eaten meats include roast lamb or beef. Wild meats like ostrich or springbok appear on restaurant menus. *Boerewors* are traditional sausages from South Africa. They are made with spiced beef mixed with lamb or pork.

CHAKALAKA

BOEREWORS

MEALIE PAP

Mealie pap is a commonly eaten dish in South Africa. Have an adult help you make this tasty recipe.

Ingredients:
6 cups vegetable or chicken stock
1 stick of butter
1 1/2 cups cornmeal
salt

Steps:

1. In a large saucepan, bring the stock to a boil.

2. Add the butter to the stock. Stir over medium heat until the butter is completely melted.

3. Gradually pour all the cornmeal into the pot. Stir it constantly. At first have the heat high so the mixture boils. Then lower the heat to medium so it thickens. After a few minutes, turn the heat to low.

4. After about 5 to 10 minutes, you will notice the pap mixture coming away from the sides of the pan. This means it is done.

5. Cover the pan and remove it from the heat. Let it rest for 15 minutes. Add salt to taste. Enjoy!

CELEBRATIONS

People in South Africa celebrate a variety of holidays. Many go to the beach on New Year's Day. Freedom Day takes place on April 27. This holiday marks when South Africa held its first **democratic** elections in 1994. Some South Africans celebrate by having a *braai*, or barbeque, with family and friends.

September 24 is Heritage Day. People celebrate the diverse mix of **cultures** in the nation. Most South Africans go to church on Christmas. They also visit relatives and give each other presents. South Africans celebrate their country and culture throughout the year!

FICKSBURG CHERRY FESTIVAL

The Ficksburg Cherry Festival occurs each November in South Africa's Free State. It is the country's longest-running crop festival. Events include live music, running races, and cherry pit-spitting contests!

HERITAGE DAY

300s
Bantu groups native to central Africa migrate to South Africa and join the native Khoikhoi and San people

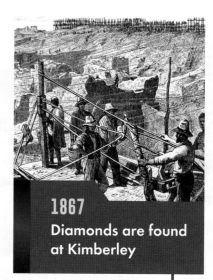

1867
Diamonds are found at Kimberley

1488
Portuguese explorer Bartholomeu Dias is the first European to sail around Africa's southern tip, opening trade routes through the area

1877
Great Britain takes control of an area of South Africa called the Transvaal

1652
The Dutch East India Company representative Jan van Riebeeck establishes the Cape Colony

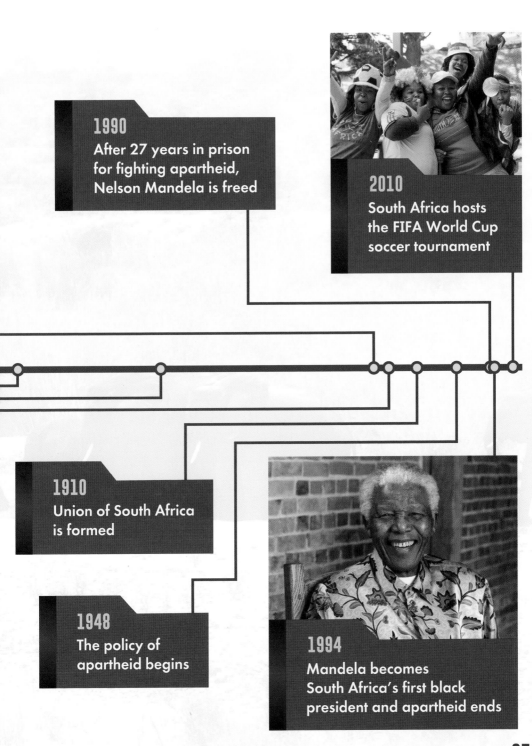

1990
After 27 years in prison for fighting apartheid, Nelson Mandela is freed

2010
South Africa hosts the FIFA World Cup soccer tournament

1910
Union of South Africa is formed

1948
The policy of apartheid begins

1994
Mandela becomes South Africa's first black president and apartheid ends

SOUTH AFRICA FACTS

Official Name: Republic of South Africa

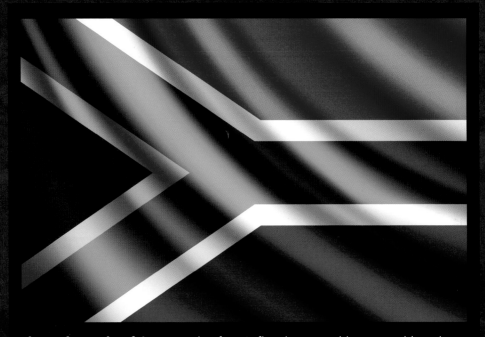

Flag of South Africa: South Africa's flag has a red horizontal band on top and a blue band on the bottom. In the middle of the flag is a green sideways Y-shaped band. Along the outer edge of the Y is a white border. Along the Y's left edge is a yellow border. A black triangle is on the flagpole side. The Y-shape represents a split road coming together for unity in the future.

Area: 470,693 square miles
(1,219,090 square kilometers)

Capital City: Bloemfontein (judicial),
Cape Town (legislative),
Pretoria (administrative)

Important Cities: Johannesburg,
Durban, Port Elizabeth

Population:
56,463,617 (July 2020)

WHERE PEOPLE LIVE

COUNTRYSIDE
32.6%

CITY
67.4%

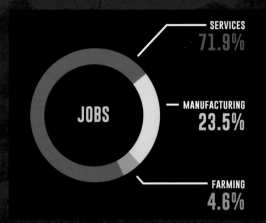

JOBS

SERVICES
71.9%

MANUFACTURING
23.5%

FARMING
4.6%

Main Exports:

gold

diamonds

platinum

cars

coal

citrus fruits

National Holiday:
Freedom Day (April 27)

Main Languages:
Zulu, Xhosa, Afrikaans, Sepedi,
Setswana, English, Sesotho, Xitsonga,
Swati, Tshivenda, Ndebele

Form of Government:
parliamentary republic

Title for Country Leader:
president

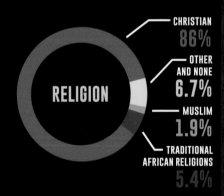

RELIGION

CHRISTIAN
86%

OTHER
AND NONE
6.7%

MUSLIM
1.9%

TRADITIONAL
AFRICAN RELIGIONS
5.4%

Unit of Money:
South African rand

GLOSSARY

apartheid—a legal system in South Africa from 1948 to 1994 that separated racial groups; during apartheid, people of color were not considered equal to white people.

cuisine—a style of cooking

cultures—the beliefs, arts, and ways of life in places or societies

democratic—related to a system of government in which people choose their leaders

diverse—made up of people or things that are different from one another

endangered—at risk of becoming extinct

escarpment—a steep slope or long cliff separating areas of land at different heights

informal settlements—densely populated areas just outside of a city which have poor living conditions and run-down housing

manufacture—to make products, often with machines

native—originally from the area or related to a group of people that began in the area

plateau—an area of flat, raised land

rural—related to the countryside

safari—an expedition to observe animals in their natural habitat

service jobs—jobs that perform tasks for people or businesses

shantytowns—areas on the outskirts of a town with large numbers of poor housing

temperate—associated with a mild climate that does not have extreme heat or cold

thatched roofs—roofs with coverings made of grass or straw

tourism—the business of people traveling to visit other places

traditional—related to customs, ideas, or beliefs handed down from one generation to the next

urban—related to cities and city life

TO LEARN MORE

AT THE LIBRARY

Krensky, Stephen. *Nelson Mandela*. New York, N.Y.: DK Publishing, 2019.

Perkins, Chloe. *Living in...South Africa*. New York, N.Y.: Simon Spotlight, 2016.

Shoup, Kate. *South Africa*. New York, N.Y.: Cavendish Square Publishing, 2018.

ON THE WEB

FACTSURFER

Factsurfer.com gives you a safe, fun way to find more information.

1. Go to www.factsurfer.com.

2. Enter "South Africa" into the search box and click 🔍.

3. Select your book cover to see a list of related content.

INDEX